Water Worlds

Sea Shores

Beth Blaxland
for the Australian Museum

This edition first published in 2002 in the United States of America by Chelsea House Publishers, a subsidiary of Haights Cross Communications

Chelsea House Publishers
1974 Sproul Road, Suite 400
Broomall, PA 19008–0914

The Chelsea House world wide web address is www.chelseahouse.com

Library of Congress Cataloging-in-Publication Data Applied for.
ISBN 0-7910-6568-5

First published in 2000 by
Macmillan Education Australia Pty Ltd
627 Chapel Street, South Yarra, Australia, 3141

Copyright © Australian Museum 2000

Australian Museum Series Editor: Carolyn MacLulich
Australian Museum Scientific Adviser: Doug Hoese
Australian Museum Publishing Unit: Jenny Saunders and Kate Lowe

Edited by Anne McKenna
Typeset in Bembo
Printed in Hong Kong
Text and cover design by Leigh Ashforth @ watershed art & design
Illustrations by Peter Mather

Acknowledgements

To my parents, Margaret and Russell,
who introduced me to the delights of the sea shore

The author and publishers are grateful to the following for permission to use copyright material:
Front cover
      Main photo: Geoffery Lea/AUSCAPE
      Inset photo: Jean-Paul Ferrero/AUSCAPE
Back cover: Jean-Paul Ferrero/AUSCAPE

Kathie Atkinson, pp. 8-9, 15 (top), 17, 26 (top), 27 (top), 27 (bottom); Brett Dennis/Lochman Transparencies, p. 5; Jean-Paul Ferrero/AUSCAPE, pp. 4, 11, 18, 19 (bottom), 20, 23 (bottom), 25; Karen Gowlett-Holmes/Oxford Scientific Films/AUSCAPE, pp. 15 (bottom), 21 (bottom); Brett Gregory/AUSCAPE, p. 24; C. Andrew Henley/AUSCAPE, pp. 6-7, 22 (top); Wayne Lawler/ AUSCAPE, p. 26 (bottom); Geoffrey Lea/AUSCAPE p. 10; Jiri Lochman/ Lochman Transparencies, pp. 12-13, 14, 16; John McCammon/AUSCAPE, pp. 3, 21 (top); Kerrie Ruth/ AUSCAPE, pp. 22 (bottom), 23 (top), 30; Dennis Sarson/Lochman Transparencies, p. 19 (top).

Contents

Sea shores and the intertidal zone

The land along the edge of the sea is called the **sea shore**, or **shore**. The sea shore looks very different from one place to another. In some places the sea shore is a sandy beach, but in other places it can be a soft mudflat, hard rocky ground or a tall cliff.

≋ These rocks on this sea shore are covered in bright green seaweed. At low tide, you can easily see the rocks and seaweed because they are not covered by water. At high tide, this sea shore looks very different because the sea covers the rocks.

The sea shore can look very different from one time to another. At high tide, the sea comes in and covers part of the shore. This is called high tide because the water comes higher up onto the shore and covers some of the land. Then, when the tide goes out, the sea water on the shore gets lower and more of the shore is uncovered. This is called low tide.

The **intertidal** (say: in-ter-ty-dal) **zone** is a very important part of the sea shore. It is the part of the sea shore that is covered by sea water at high tide and uncovered at low tide. It is the only part of the Earth that belongs to both the sea and the land.

This part of the shore is always covered by the sea, even at low tide. It is not part of the intertidal zone.

This part of the shore is never covered by the sea, even at high tide. It is not part of the intertidal zone.

This part of the shore is covered by the sea at high tide and uncovered at low tide. It is in the intertidal zone.

Tides

The intertidal zone is the place where the level of the water on the shore is always changing. A high tide is always followed by a low tide and a low tide is always followed by another high tide. Most places have two high tides and two low tides each day but some only get one high tide and one low tide each day.

≋ It is low tide on this sea shore but the brown seaweed that has been washed up shows how much of the shore was covered by the last high tide. When the next high tide comes in, some of this seaweed might get washed back out to sea.

On some shores, the high tide comes in a long way and the low tide goes out a long way. These shores have wide intertidal zones. On other shores, the tides only come in and go out a short way. These shores have narrow intertidal zones.

Wide and narrow intertidal zones are often caused by the shape of the shore. Wide intertidal zones are found on flat shores. Some very wide intertidal zones are more than two kilometers (1.2 miles) wide. Narrow intertidal zones are often found on steep shores and can be less than one meter (3 feet) wide.

This intertidal zone is quite wide but it is not as wide as some. If this sea shore was flatter, its intertidal zone would be even wider.

Did you know?

Some high tides are higher than others and some low tides are lower than others. These changes are caused by the moon.

The moon pulls the water in the oceans up towards it and makes the water bulge upwards. About every two weeks there is a full moon or a new moon. When this happens, the pull on the water is greater and this makes the high tide come higher up the shore and the low tide go further down the shore.

Waves

In many places, waves crash onto the seashore. Waves are made by the wind as it blows across the sea. At first, the wind makes little ripples that get bigger and turn into small waves. If the wind keeps blowing, the waves get bigger and bigger. Strong winds can make these waves even bigger.

When the waves reach shallow water, they curl over and crash onto the shore. When the high tide comes in, the waves crash onto the higher parts of the intertidal zone. Then, as the tide goes out, the waves crash onto lower parts of the intertidal zone.

Waves can wash beach sand away or move it to other parts of the shore. When sand or bits of rock are mixed in with the waves, they get thrown against the shore with the crashing waves. This wears the shore away even more.

Did you know?

Sometimes the waves crashing onto the shore are much bigger than usual. These big waves are caused by storms with very strong winds. Sometimes the storm is near the shore, but often it is way out at sea where you cannot see it.

Big waves made by storms out at sea can travel for days before they reach the shore. By the time they reach the shore, they are very big and powerful. These waves are so powerful, they crash higher up on the shore than usual.

≋ Rocky shores often get a lot of waves. The waves slowly wear down the rock, carrying tiny bits of rock away to be washed up onto other shores where they make beaches.

Sea shore habitats

A **habitat** is the place where something lives. Some sea shore habitats are:
- sheltered shores
- sandy shores with waves
- rocky shores with waves
- rock pools.

Sheltered shores

Sheltered shores are protected from the open ocean and do not get big waves. Bays and **estuaries** (say: est-shu-reez) have sheltered shores. Estuaries are places near the sea where fresh water from a river mixes with salty water from the sea. Sheltered shores are also found where coral reefs form a barrier that stops big ocean waves getting through to the shore.

The ground in these habitats is mostly made of soft mud or loose sand. This mud and sand is washed onto the shore by rivers and the tides from the sea. The mud and sand stay on sheltered shores because there are no big waves to wash them away. Many plants and animals live on sheltered shores.

≋ This is a sheltered shore habitat. There are no waves to crash onto the shore and wash the sand away.

sandy shore
with waves

rocky shore

rock pool

≋ This picture shows three different sea shore habitats.

Sandy shores with waves

When waves break on sandy shores, they stir up the sand. Plants and animals that live in this habitat can be crushed by waves, buried under moving sand or washed out to sea.

Rocky shores with waves

Some rocks are harder than other rocks. When waves crash onto rocks, they slowly wear away the softer bits of rock. This makes cracks and holes in the rocky shore. Sometimes chunks of rock are broken off and smashed onto the shore by the waves. Many plants and animals live on the rocks in this habitat but the waves can injure them.

Rock pools

Sometimes rock pools are found on rocky shores. Some rock pools are very shallow and dry up at low tide on hot days. Others are very deep and are always filled with sea water. Rock pools are a habitat for many living things.

Life on sheltered shores

Anything that lives on the sea shore must be **adapted** to living there. When plants and animals are adapted to their habitat, they are suited to their surroundings and can easily live and grow in that place. A living thing that spends all of its life in one habitat also needs to be able to reproduce there.

≋ The plants in this picture are mangroves. When high tide comes in, these mangroves will be flooded by sea water.

Look closely and you will see many dark mud whelks on the mud. Mud whelks are sea snails that have long pointed shells. They feed on rotting mangrove leaves and tiny algae growing on the mud.

Plants

The intertidal zone on sheltered shores has soft, wet ground that is flooded by sea water for part of each day. Only a few kinds of plants can grow in this habitat. Two kinds of plants that are adapted to living here are mangrove trees and some tiny **algae** (say: al-gee). Algae are very simple plants, such as seaweeds, that do not have leaves, stems or roots like other plants.

Mangroves only grow and reproduce on sheltered shores. They do not grow on shores with strong waves because the waves would push the mangroves over and wash them away. Mangroves reproduce by making seeds that grow into new mangrove plants. The seeds start growing while they are still on the parent mangrove tree. Then they drop off the tree and float away in the high tide. After a while, they stop floating and grow roots in the mud.

≋ You can see many young mangrove plants growing in the mud. They have grown from seeds made by the mangrove trees in the background.

Plants need oxygen to live. If a plant's roots cannot get enough oxygen, the whole plant will die. Mangroves grow in wet ground that does not have much oxygen in it. They can live there because they have special roots that grow upwards, to get oxygen from the air.

Look for the mangroves' above-ground roots in this picture. They grow up out of the mud and look like little sticks without leaves.

Animals

Many animals are adapted to living on sheltered shores. Many of these animals live on or under the ground. For example, sea worms burrow underground and mud whelks and other sea snails crawl over the ground. Shore birds, called **waders**, wade in the water or walk on the ground looking for these small animals to eat.

At low tide, crabs come out of their burrows to feed. Many small crabs feed on **detritus** (say: de-tri-tus). Detritus is food made up of plants or animals that have rotted away into tiny bits. This food gets washed onto the shore at high tide and mixed in with the sand or mud.

Other animals, such as fishes and prawns, swim in at high tide and swim out again before low tide. Many of these animals use sheltered shores as a nursery area for their young.

These little balls of sand show where the crab has been feeding. It takes a mouthful of sand and detritus from the ground, eats the detritus and then spits the sand back onto the beach.

This is the entrance to a crab's burrow. Crabs use these burrows to hide from fishes and birds that might want to eat them.

Many animals that live in the sea have a shell. The shell protects the soft body of the animal that lives inside. Empty shells washed up onto the shore are from animals that have died.

Most shelled animals have one or two shells. Sea snails have one shell that curls around their bodies. They come in many shapes, sizes and colors.

Animals that have two shells are called **bivalves** (say: by-valvz). These two shells are joined together along one side and the whole shell can open and close like the cover of a book. The body of the bivalve lies in between the two shells.

This bubble shell is a kind of sea snail. It crawls on and burrows in the soft ground of sheltered shores.

sea snail

These big pink frills are part of the bubble shell's soft body. They stop mud and sand getting in the animal's shell when it burrows. Bubble shells eat bivalves and other sea snails.

This cockle is a bivalve. You can see one of its shells and also part of its soft body poking out from under the shell. Some bivalves, like this one, burrow into the ground. They have a strong foot that they use to dig down into the soft ground.

bivalve

Life on sandy shores with waves

Sandy shores with waves are habitats where loose sand on the shore gets stirred up by waves. The sand is always moving about and large plants cannot live in this moving ground. The only plants that can live here are tiny algae that are smaller than a grain of sand.

Most of the animals that live here are hard to see because they burrow into the sand or swim in at high tide. Only a few animals live above ground in this habitat.

Ghost crabs are hard to see because they are almost the same color as the sand and they run away very quickly.

Did you know?

Crabs can crawl slowly forwards, but when they want to move quickly, most crabs crawl or run sideways. Ghost crabs can move very quickly when they run sideways. They can run faster than most other crabs.

≋ Ghost crabs make deep burrows in the sand near the top of the shore. They stay in their burrows during the day to hide from seagulls and other animals that might eat them. At night they come out to look for food in the intertidal zone. They hunt for small animals such as bivalves and small crabs.

Some of the animals in this habitat are bivalves that burrow in the sand below the waves. These bivalves have tough shells to protect them from being hurt by the waves. Pipis (say: pi-pees) are bivalves that live just below the sand on many beaches with waves. The waves sometimes wash them out of the sand but they quickly burrow back down again. Pipis are **filter feeders**. This means they feed by sifting very tiny plants and animals out of the water. These very tiny plants and animals are called **plankton**.

To help them feed, pipis have two tubes that they stretch out into the water. You can see these tubes here. They use one tube to suck water and plankton inside their bodies. Then they filter the plankton out of the water and use the other tube to let the water back out.

≋ Pipis are eaten by sea birds, sea worms and some people. People also catch pipis to use as bait when they go fishing.

Did you know?

Beachworms are a kind of sea worm. They live under the sand of beaches. Giant Beachworms can grow to two meters (6.5 feet) long. They eat young pipis and other small bivalves. Some people catch beachworms to use as bait.

Flotsam and jetsam

High tides and waves wash a lot of things up onto sandy beaches. This is called **flotsam and jetsam**. Some of the things washed up are natural, such as seaweeds, shells and many kinds of small sea animals that can be dead or alive. Other things are made by people, such as fishing line, rope, timber and many kinds of plastic including bags, bottles and bottle tops.

Look at this flotsam and jetsam. How much of it is natural and how much is rubbish made by people?

Flotsam and jetsam can give shelter to small sea shore animals such as the red crabs in this picture.

Some animals also find food washed up in the flotsam and jetsam. Some flotsam and jetsam can be dangerous to animals living in this habitat. For example, animals can get tangled in fishing line or can eat plastic by mistake.

Birds

Many kinds of birds live on sandy shores with waves.
They use the shore as a place to rest and feed.

≋ Many of the birds on sandy shores are waders. Waders are often found on sheltered shores where they wade in the water looking for food buried in the mud or sand. Waders can also be found on sandy shores with waves. Sometimes they look for food such as sea worms or bivalves, but most of the time they are just resting.

≋ Seagulls and other sea birds also rest on these shores. Sometimes they fly near the shore and swoop down to the water to catch fish. Seagulls also search the flotsam and jetsam for dead fish or other food washed onto the shore.

Life on rocky shores with waves

Rocky shores with waves are habitats that do not have soft ground for plants to grow in or animals to burrow into. Instead, the living things in this habitat live on the surface of the rocks. These plants and animals are adapted so they can hold onto the rocks, even when waves crash onto them.

Plants

Many large algae plants are found on rocky shores. They are seaweeds that tightly grip the rocks using **holdfasts** that look like little fingers. At low tide, many small animals shelter under the seaweeds.

The middle part of the intertidal zone often has a lot of seaweeds. One kind of seaweed found here is called Neptune's Necklace. It is called Neptune's Necklace because Neptune is the name of the ancient Roman god of the sea and this seaweed looks like strings of round beads from a necklace.

Large seaweeds called kelp grow on rocky shores on the lowest part of the intertidal zone.

Neptune's Necklace

Tiny algae plants also grow on the rocks. Some kinds of tiny algae are very slippery to walk on. Others are very hard and feel like rock. Algae is eaten by many **invertebrate** (say: in–ver–ter–brait) animals that live on the rocks. Invertebrate animals are animals that do not have a backbone. They include sea snails, worms and crabs.

The dark red-brown colored scum on this rock is algae. It is eaten by some sea snails and other small animals.

Some kinds of algae look like pink or red paint on the rocks. This algae feels hard and stony if you touch it.

This is a chiton (say: kite-on) or coat-of-mail shell. Chitons are invertebrates that crawl about like sea snails and eat tiny algae growing on the rocks. When the tide is out, they often shelter under large seaweeds or in cracks in the rocks.

Animals

Most animals living in this sea shore habitat are sea animals. They can dry out and die if they are out of the water for too long, so they need to be adapted to living in a habitat where the tide goes out.

Many animals living on rocky shores have a shell they can shut at low tide to stop them drying out. They wait until the tide comes back in again before they open their shell to feed and move about under the water.

≋ At low tide, limpets pull their shells down onto the rock so that they will not dry out. When the tide covers them again, they lift their shells and move about to feed on tiny algae.

Sea-squirts hold tightly onto rocks at the bottom of the intertidal zone. They do not have a shell to protect them from drying out at low tide. Instead, they keep themselves wet when the tide goes out by storing water inside their bodies. If you touch them, they will squirt the water out.

Sea-squirts are filter feeders. They suck water in through the cross-shaped holes at the top of their bodies. Tiny plant and animal plankton are filtered out of this water and eaten, then the water is let back out.

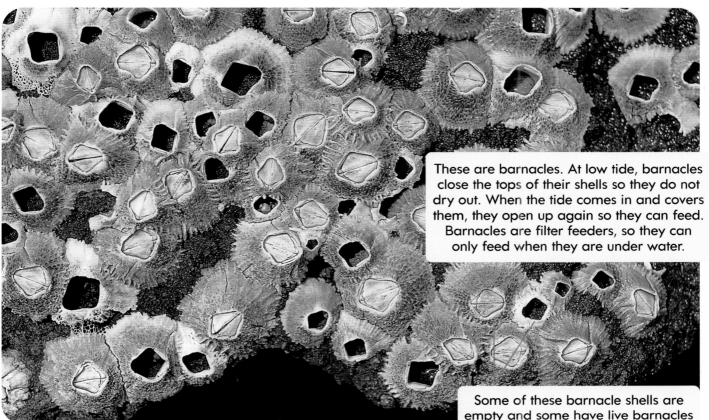

These are barnacles. At low tide, barnacles close the tops of their shells so they do not dry out. When the tide comes in and covers them, they open up again so they can feed. Barnacles are filter feeders, so they can only feed when they are under water.

Some of these barnacle shells are empty and some have live barnacles in them. The shells of the living barnacles are closed at the top because it is low tide. The empty shells are open at the top. Empty shells belong to barnacles that have died. The barnacles that used to live in these empty shells may have been eaten by another animal.

≋ These little black sea snails are called Mulberry Whelks because their shells look a bit like mulberries. They eat barnacles, bivalves and other sea snails. The sea snails in this picture are feeding on oysters. Oysters are a kind of bivalve that grows on rocks and other hard surfaces.

Mulberry Whelks crawl onto an animal's shell and scrape a hole through the shell to get to the soft animal inside.

Life in rock pools

Rock pools are sometimes found on rocky shores. They are a special kind of sea shore habitat because they are wetter than the surrounding rocky shore at low tide.

Shallow rock pools hold only a little bit of water. On hot days, this water can get very hot and evaporate, or dry out. Only a few things can live in shallow rock pools.

Deep rock pools always have water in them. Many things live in deep rock pools. Some plants and animals live there all the time but some animals only move into rock pools at low tide so they can stay wet while the rest of the shore is dry.

≋ At high tide, this rocky shore and rock pool were covered by water. Now it is low tide and the rock pool is still filled with water, but the rest of the shore is dry.

This deep rock pool is a habitat for many plants and animals. Large seaweeds and many tiny algae plants grow on the sides of this rock pool. Invertebrate animals shelter under the seaweeds and small fishes swim about.

Some sea snails live on rocky shores at high tide then move into rock pools at low tide when the rest of the shore is dry. They move into rock pools at low tide so that they can keep feeding under the water. Other sea snails that do not move into rock pools cannot keep feeding because they have to shut their shells at low tide so they do not dry out.

Did you know?

Sea snails and chitons have special tongues that help them eat. These tongues are covered with tiny teeth. Sea snails that eat algae rub their tongues over the rock to scrape the algae off. Sea snails that eat bivalves or other sea snails rub their tongues over an animal's shell to scrape a hole in the shell. Then they eat the animal inside.

≋ These sea snails are called Zebra Periwinkles. They move into rock pools at low tide so that they can feed on tiny algae. There are a lot of dark brown algae on this rock for the Zebra Periwinkles to eat.

Some animals settle in a rock pool and then stay in the one place to feed. Two animals that do this are tube worms and sea anemones (say: a-ne-mo-neez).

Tube worms are sea worms that live in long tubes that they make and never leave. They stick their tubes onto the rocks and use them like burrows.

Sea anemones can slowly move about, but when they are feeding, they grip onto the rocks and wait for food to come to them.

Tube worms are filter feeders. They stretch out their long tentacles that look like feathers. These tentacles filter tiny plankton out of the water for the tube worm to eat.

Some tubes, like this one, look empty. The tube worm that made this tube might be hiding inside to escape danger.

Sea anemones use their tentacles to catch small animals that come near them. They feed on small animals, such as sea worms, shrimp and fishes. Sea anemones are eaten by big fishes and sea stars.

Other animals move about to search for food. Sometimes they even move out of one rock pool and into another. Two animals that do this are sea stars and octopuses.

Sea stars look for food in deep rock pools and shady parts of the shore. Most sea stars eat bivalves and sea snails. Sea stars' mouths are underneath their bodies so they have to crawl on top of their food to eat it.

Octopuses hunt in rock pools for crabs, bivalves and sea snails to eat.

≋ Some sea stars have colors that make them hard to see. There are four sea stars here. Which ones are the hardest to see? Those that are easy to see get eaten by fishes.

This octopus is feeding on a crab. Crabs hide in cracks in the rocks but octopuses have long arms to reach them.

Octopuses can change color to match the rocks they are near. This helps them hide from big fishes that like to eat them.

Food web of the sea shore

A food web shows what the different living things in a habitat eat. Plants are always at the beginning of a food web. The plants in some sea shore habitats include mangrove trees and algae.

Many of the animals in a habitat eat plants. Living things that eat plants are called **herbivores** (say: her-bi-vorz).

Some living things eat animals. Often a big animal eats a small one. Living things that eat animals are called **carnivores** (say: kar-ni-vorz).

Some living things eat plants and animals. These living things are called **omnivores** (say: om-ni-vorz).

Many of the living things in sheltered shore habitats eat detritus. These living things are called **detrivores** (say: de-tri-vorz).

≋ This food web only shows some of the plants and animals that live in sea shore habitats. Where would you add in other living things such as bubble shells, chitons, sea stars or Giant Beachworms?

Plants and detritus

plant plankton in the water

algae on the shore

detritus from mangrove trees

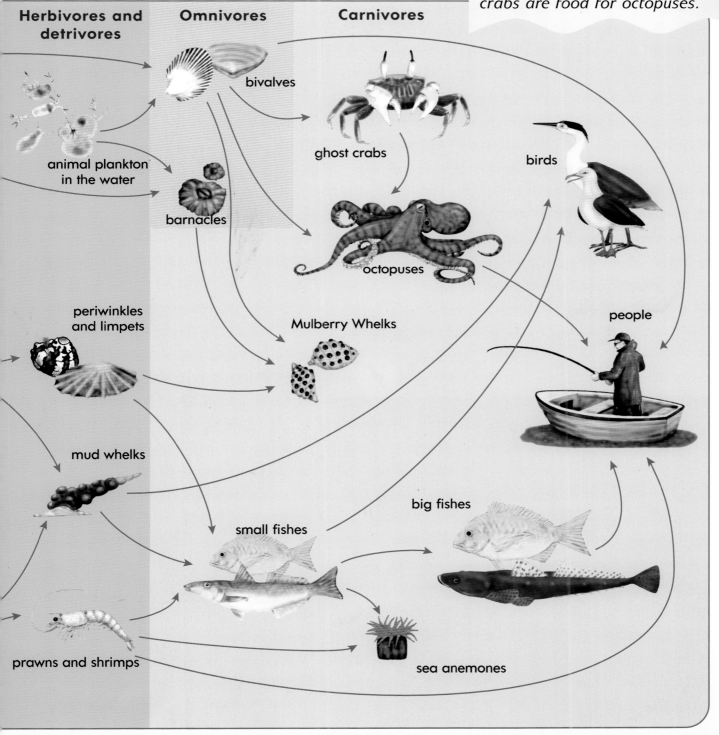

Did you know?

In a food web, arrows point from the food to the living thing that eats it.

For example:

ghost crabs ──────→ octopuses

This means that ghost crabs are eaten by octopuses, or that ghost crabs are food for octopuses.

Herbivores and detrivores

Omnivores

Carnivores

bivalves

animal plankton in the water

barnacles

ghost crabs

birds

octopuses

periwinkles and limpets

Mulberry Whelks

people

mud whelks

big fishes

small fishes

prawns and shrimps

sea anemones

Environment watch

Why is the sea shore important?

Sea shore habitats are important because:

- They are part land and part sea. This makes them special places where living things from both the land and the sea are found.
- Many living things use them for shelter. For example, some animals shelter under seaweeds, others burrow under the ground and others shelter in cracks in the rocks.
- They are used by living things as a place to reproduce. For example, prawns and fishes use the intertidal zone as nursery areas for their young.
- Many living things find food there.
- They provide food such as fish for people. They also provide plants and animals that people use as bait when they go fishing.

Things You Can Do
to help protect the sea shore

- When you visit the sea shore, be careful what you walk on and try not to damage anything.
- If you move any plants or animals, always return them to exactly the same place you found them. Otherwise they might die.
- Do not leave any rubbish behind, especially fishing lines, as these can be dangerous for the animals living there.
- Talk about the sea shore with your friends and family. Let them know why it is important and how they can help protect it.

Glossary

adapted	when a living thing is used to a special habitat and can easily live there
algae	plants, such as seaweeds, that live in wet conditions and do not have leaves, stems or roots
bivalves	invertebrate animals with two shells, such as clams, cockles, pipis, mussels and oysters
carnivores	living things that eat animals
detritus	food made up of plants and animals that have rotted away into tiny pieces
detrivores	living things that eat detritus
estuaries	places where fresh water from a river mixes with salty water from the sea
filter feeders	animals that eat by filtering out plankton and other tiny pieces of food from the water around them
flotsam and jetsam	things washed up onto the shore by the high tide and waves. Some things are natural, such as seaweeds and shells; and some are made by people, such as litter and plastic.
habitat	the place where a living thing lives. For example, mud whelks live on sheltered shores.
herbivores	living things that eat plants
holdfasts	the parts of seaweeds that grip onto the rocks so the seaweeds do not get washed away
intertidal zone	the area on the seashore or the bank of an estuary that is covered by water at high tide and uncovered at low tide
invertebrate	an animal that does not have a backbone, such as snails, crabs, prawns and worms
omnivores	living things that eat plants and animals
plankton	very tiny plants and animals that float in the sea
sea shore	the land along the edge of the sea
shore	the land along the edge of a sea, lake or river
waders	shore birds that wade in the water or walk on the shore looking for small fishes and invertebrate animals to eat

Index